GOD'S WONDERFUL WORLD
COLOURING BOOK

F I S H

1 The **clown wrasse** *(Coris gaimard)* lives with other beautiful fish among the reefs of the Philippine Islands. It makes its home in caves, or shells or a cleft in the rock. If the water gets very cool at night, it wriggles down into the sand for warmth.

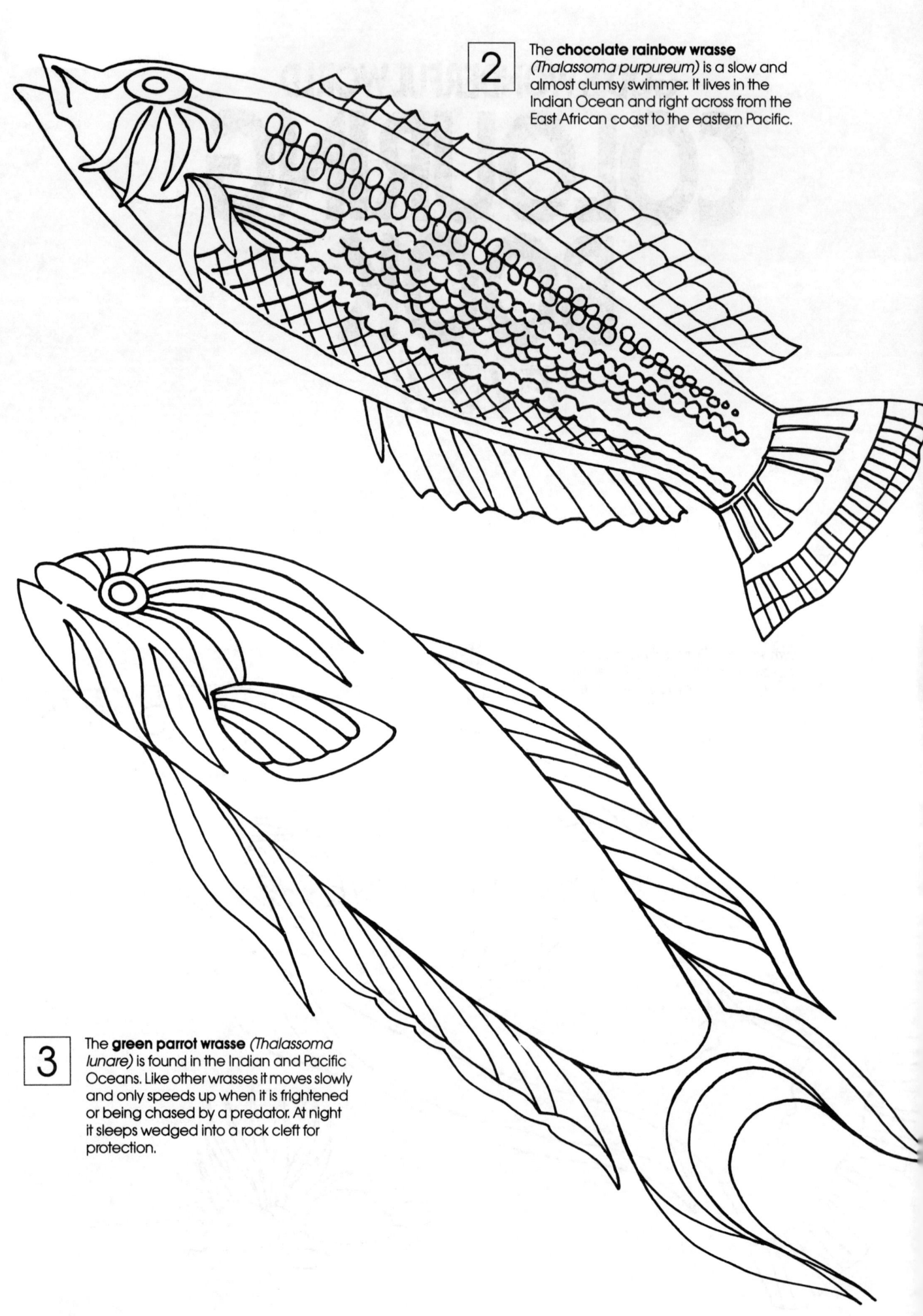

2 The **chocolate rainbow wrasse** (*Thalassoma purpureum*) is a slow and almost clumsy swimmer. It lives in the Indian Ocean and right across from the East African coast to the eastern Pacific.

3 The **green parrot wrasse** (*Thalassoma lunare*) is found in the Indian and Pacific Oceans. Like other wrasses it moves slowly and only speeds up when it is frightened or being chased by a predator. At night it sleeps wedged into a rock cleft for protection.

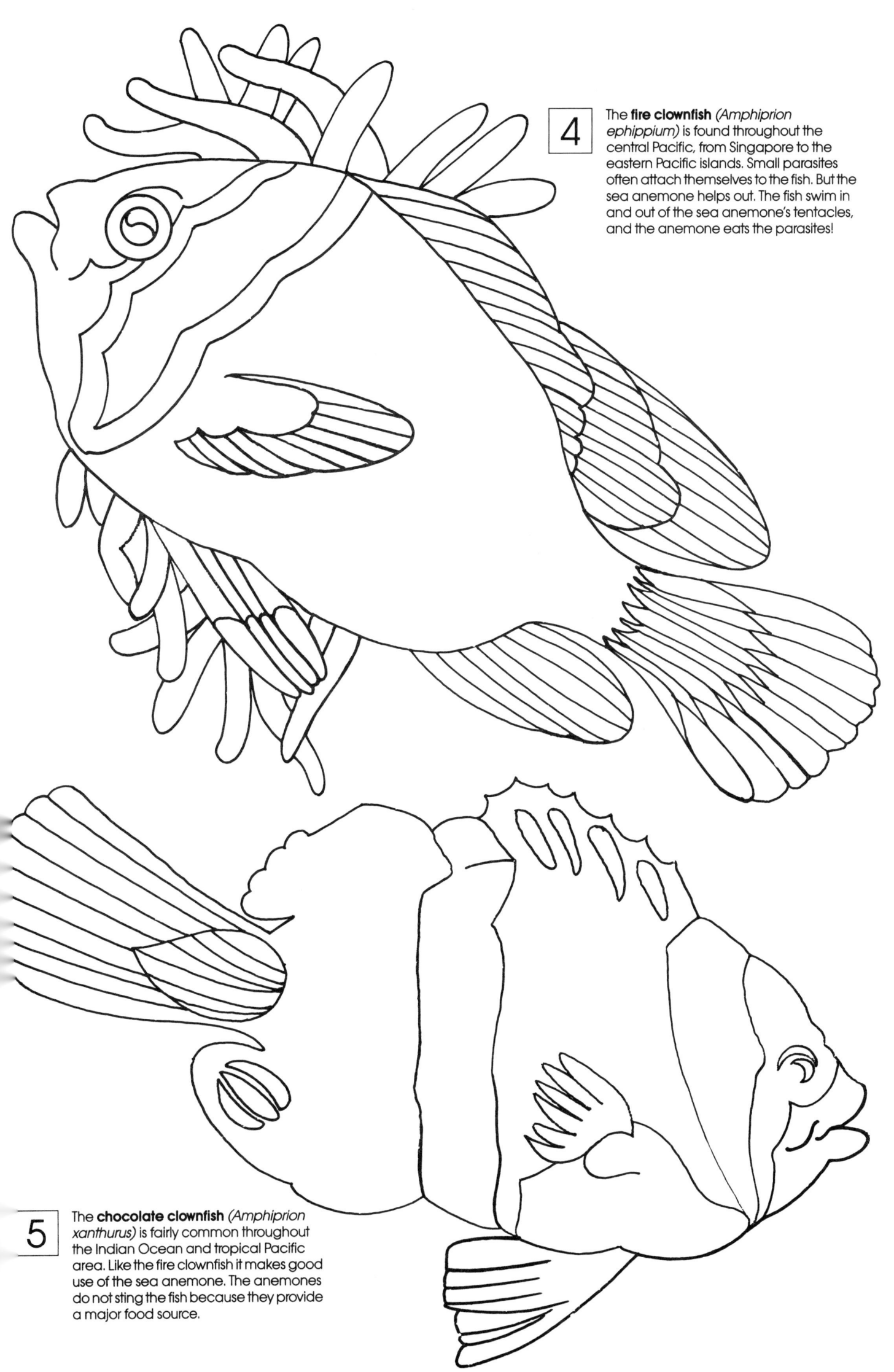

4 The **fire clownfish** (*Amphiprion ephippium*) is found throughout the central Pacific, from Singapore to the eastern Pacific islands. Small parasites often attach themselves to the fish. But the sea anemone helps out. The fish swim in and out of the sea anemone's tentacles, and the anemone eats the parasites!

5 The **chocolate clownfish** (*Amphiprion xanthurus*) is fairly common throughout the Indian Ocean and tropical Pacific area. Like the fire clownfish it makes good use of the sea anemone. The anemones do not sting the fish because they provide a major food source.

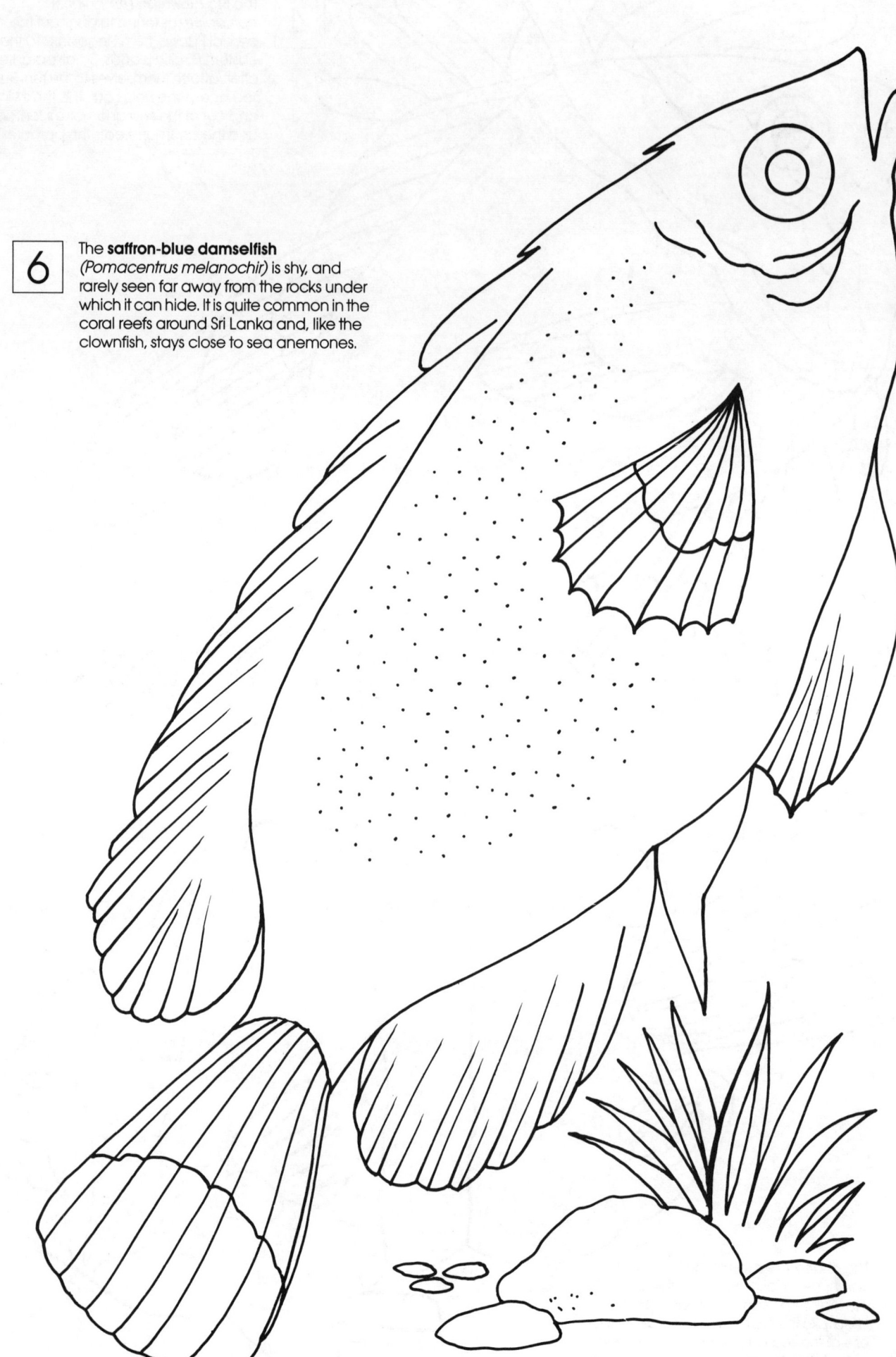

6 The **saffron-blue damselfish** (*Pomacentrus melanochir*) is shy, and rarely seen far away from the rocks under which it can hide. It is quite common in the coral reefs around Sri Lanka and, like the clownfish, stays close to sea anemones.

7 The **spotted sweetlips** (*Gaterin lineatus*) lives near coral reefs in the eastern Pacific.

8 The **green forktail damselfish** (*Chromis cyanae*) also lives near coral reefs in the Pacific Ocean. Schools of about fifty fish gather by a reef facing into the current. Every now and then they dart out to capture some morsel of tasty plankton to eat.

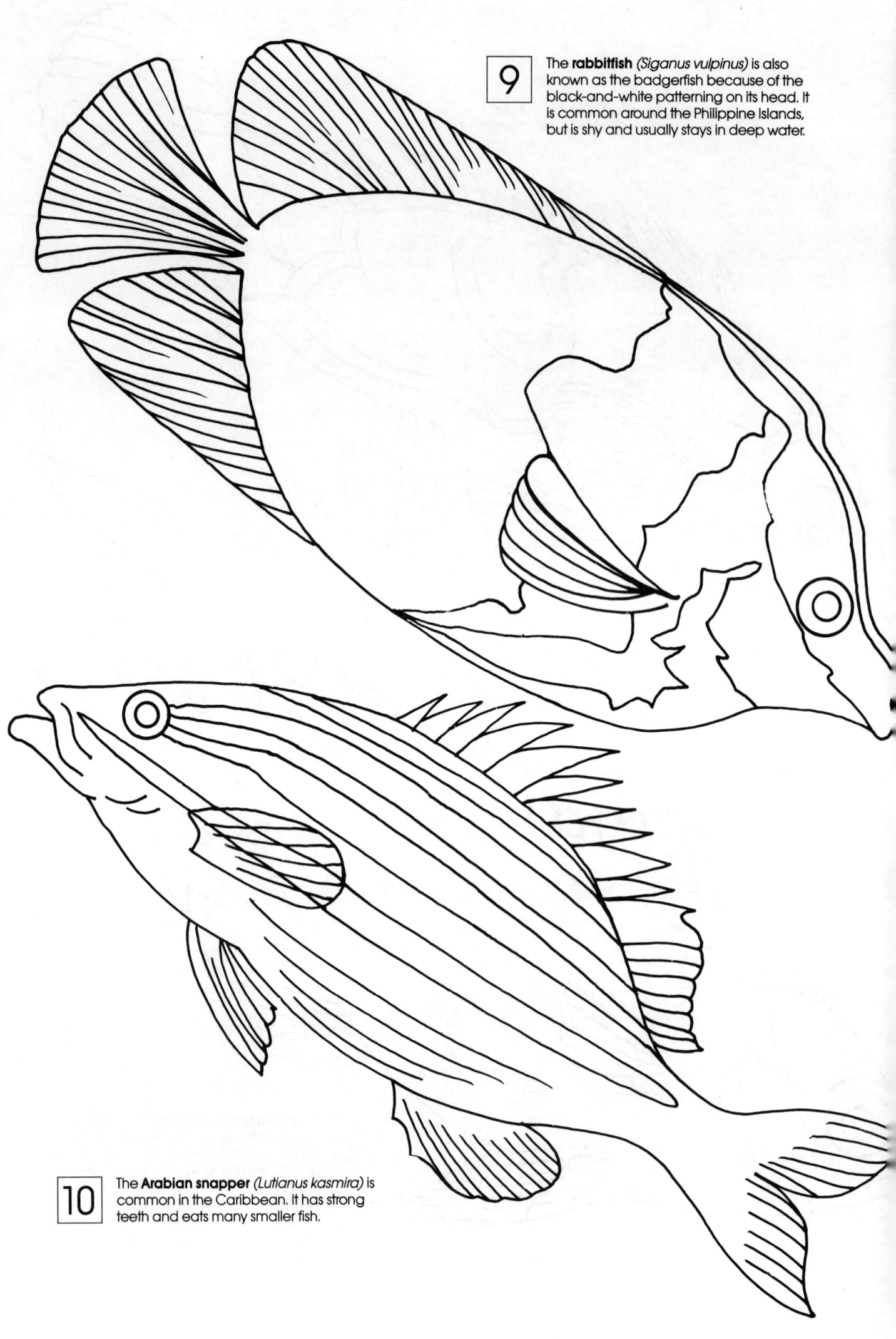

9 The **rabbitfish** (*Siganus vulpinus*) is also known as the badgerfish because of the black-and-white patterning on its head. It is common around the Philippine Islands, but is shy and usually stays in deep water.

10 The **Arabian snapper** (*Lutianus kasmira*) is common in the Caribbean. It has strong teeth and eats many smaller fish.

11 The **powder-blue surgeonfish** (*Acanthurus leucosternon*) is most common in the Indian and Pacific Oceans. It has a sharp spine which can be raised at right angles to the fish's body as a useful weapon.

12 The **dwarf angelfish** (*Centropyge argus*) lives only in the Caribbean. Even there you would be lucky to see it, as it usually swims at least 30m (almost 100 ft) below the surface.

13 The beautiful **queen angelfish** (*Holocanthus isabelita*) is found only in the Caribbean area. Like all angelfish it has a razor-sharp curved spine on the base of each gill cover. When fighting, it raises these spines and uses them to slash the enemy.

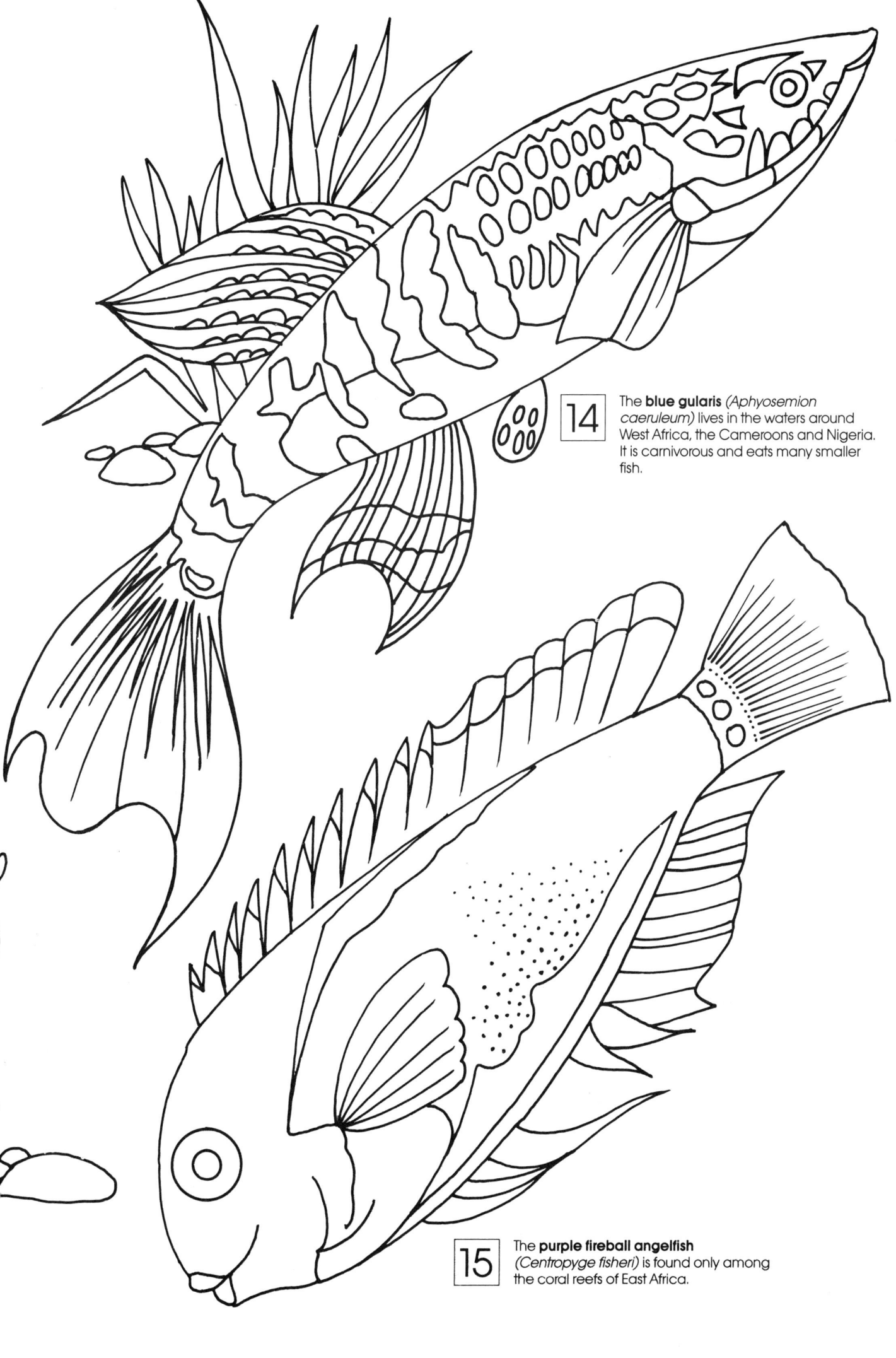

14 The **blue gularis** (*Aphyosemion caeruleum*) lives in the waters around West Africa, the Cameroons and Nigeria. It is carnivorous and eats many smaller fish.

15 The **purple fireball angelfish** (*Centropyge fisheri*) is found only among the coral reefs of East Africa.

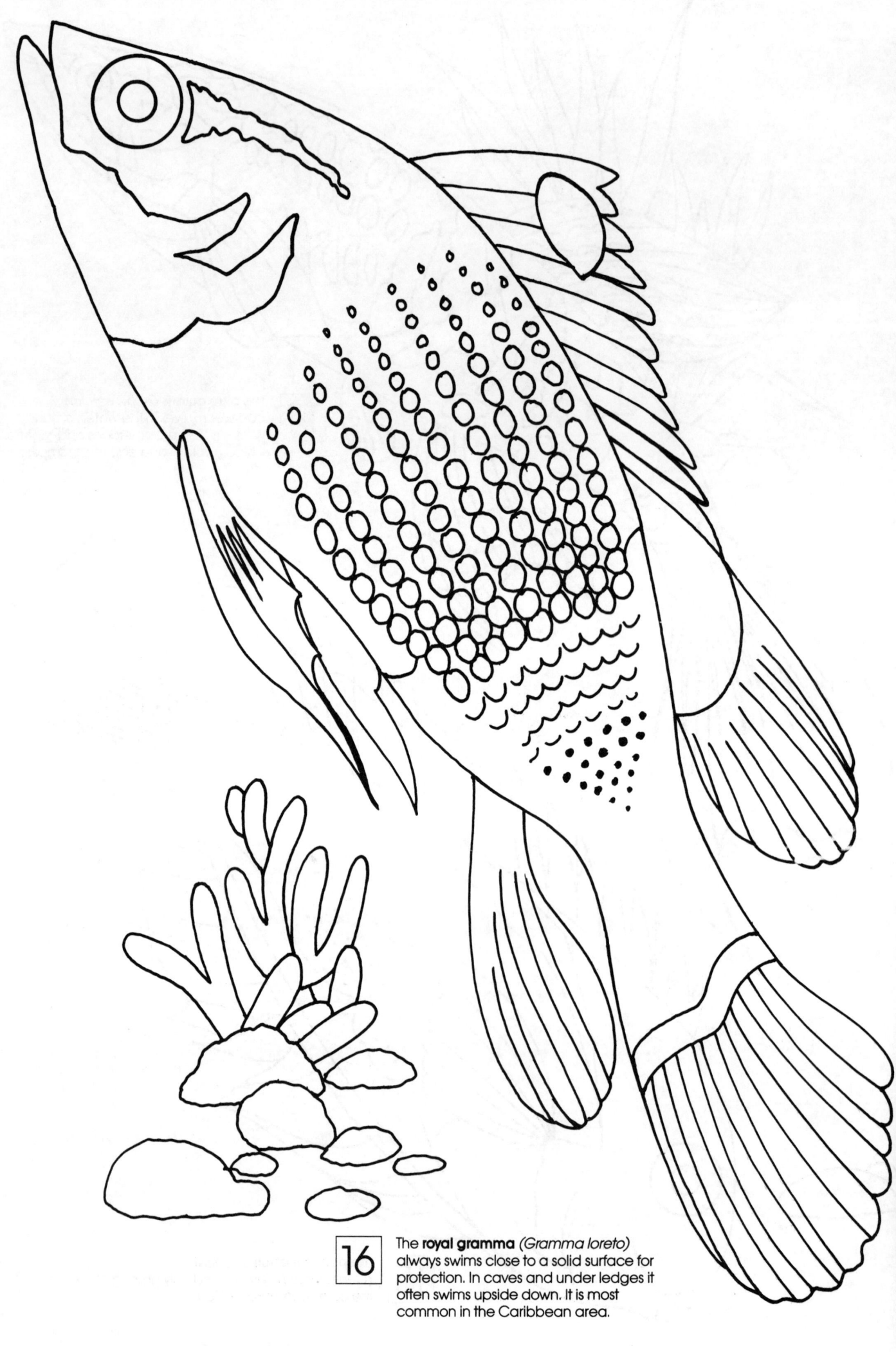

16   The **royal gramma** (*Gramma loreto*) always swims close to a solid surface for protection. In caves and under ledges it often swims upside down. It is most common in the Caribbean area.

17 The **regal tang** (*Paracanthurus theutis*) has been described as 'the bluest thing on earth'. It is a sociable fish, living in schools among the reefs of the Philippines.

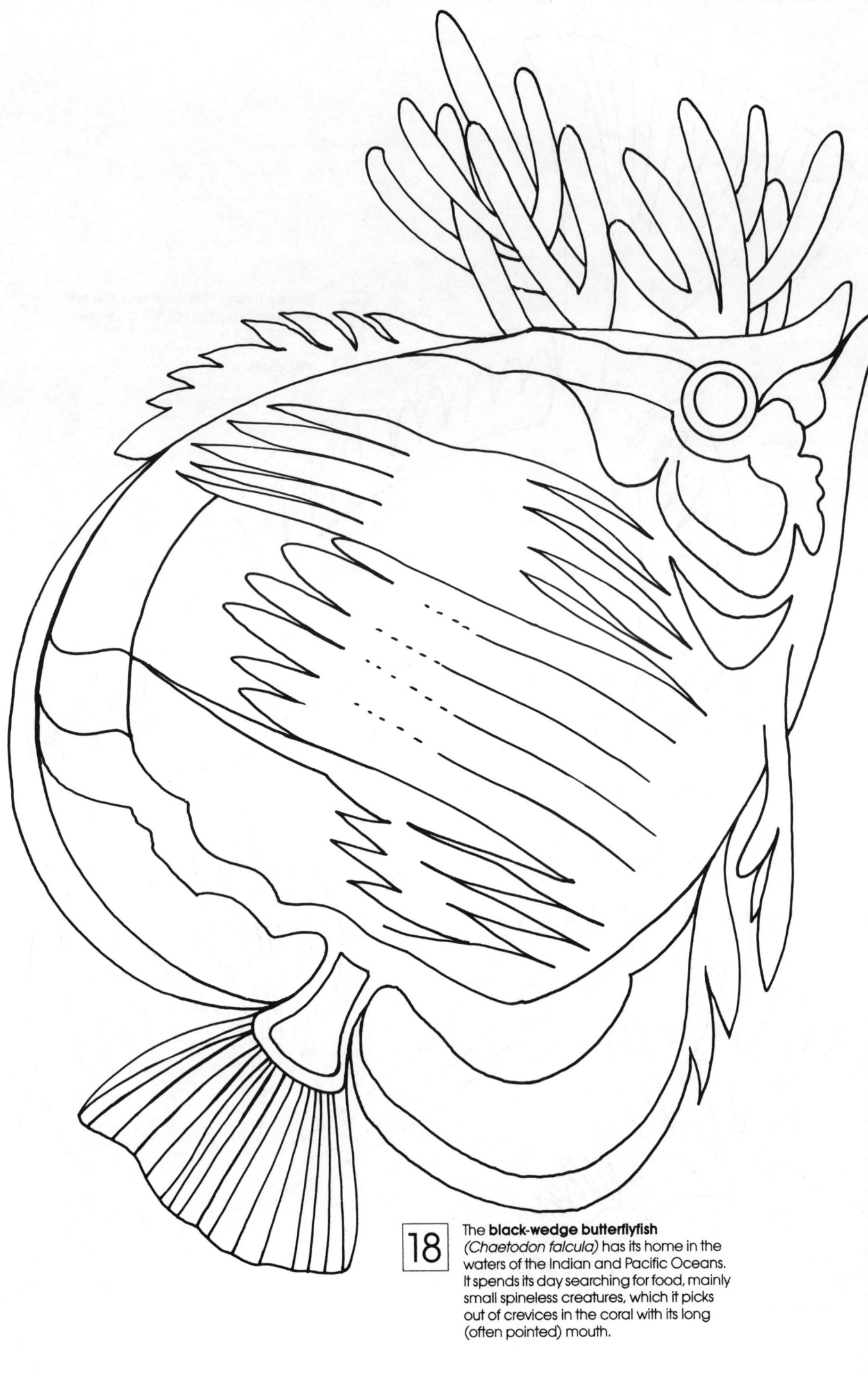

18 The **black-wedge butterflyfish**
(*Chaetodon falcula*) has its home in the
waters of the Indian and Pacific Oceans.
It spends its day searching for food, mainly
small spineless creatures, which it picks
out of crevices in the coral with its long
(often pointed) mouth.

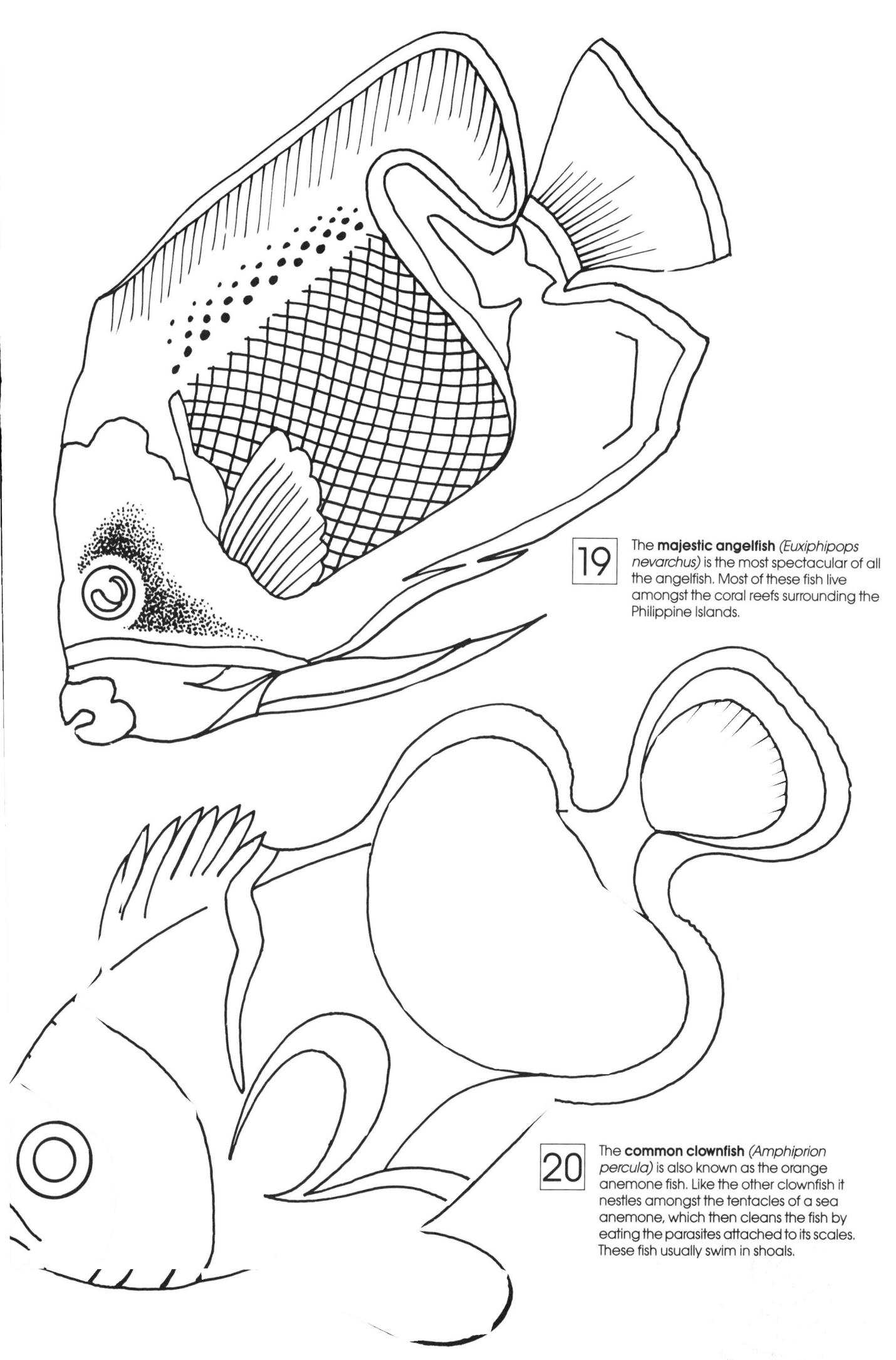

19 The **majestic angelfish** *(Euxiphipops nevarchus)* is the most spectacular of all the angelfish. Most of these fish live amongst the coral reefs surrounding the Philippine Islands.

20 The **common clownfish** *(Amphiprion percula)* is also known as the orange anemone fish. Like the other clownfish it nestles amongst the tentacles of a sea anemone, which then cleans the fish by eating the parasites attached to its scales. These fish usually swim in shoals.

21

21 The **Cuban hogfish** (*Bodianus pulchellus*) prefers deep waters where it appears to be mainly red. However, in shallow water it may change to a mixture of green and red.

22 The **soldierfish** (*Holocentrus xantherythrus*) is active mainly at night – hence its large eyes. It spends the day hidden in a rock crevice. It is a predator and can move at lightning speed to seize its prey. But at other times it is not a very energetic swimmer.

23 The **chequered angelfish** *(Holocanthus xanthurus)* comes from the coral reefs off the shores of Sri Lanka.

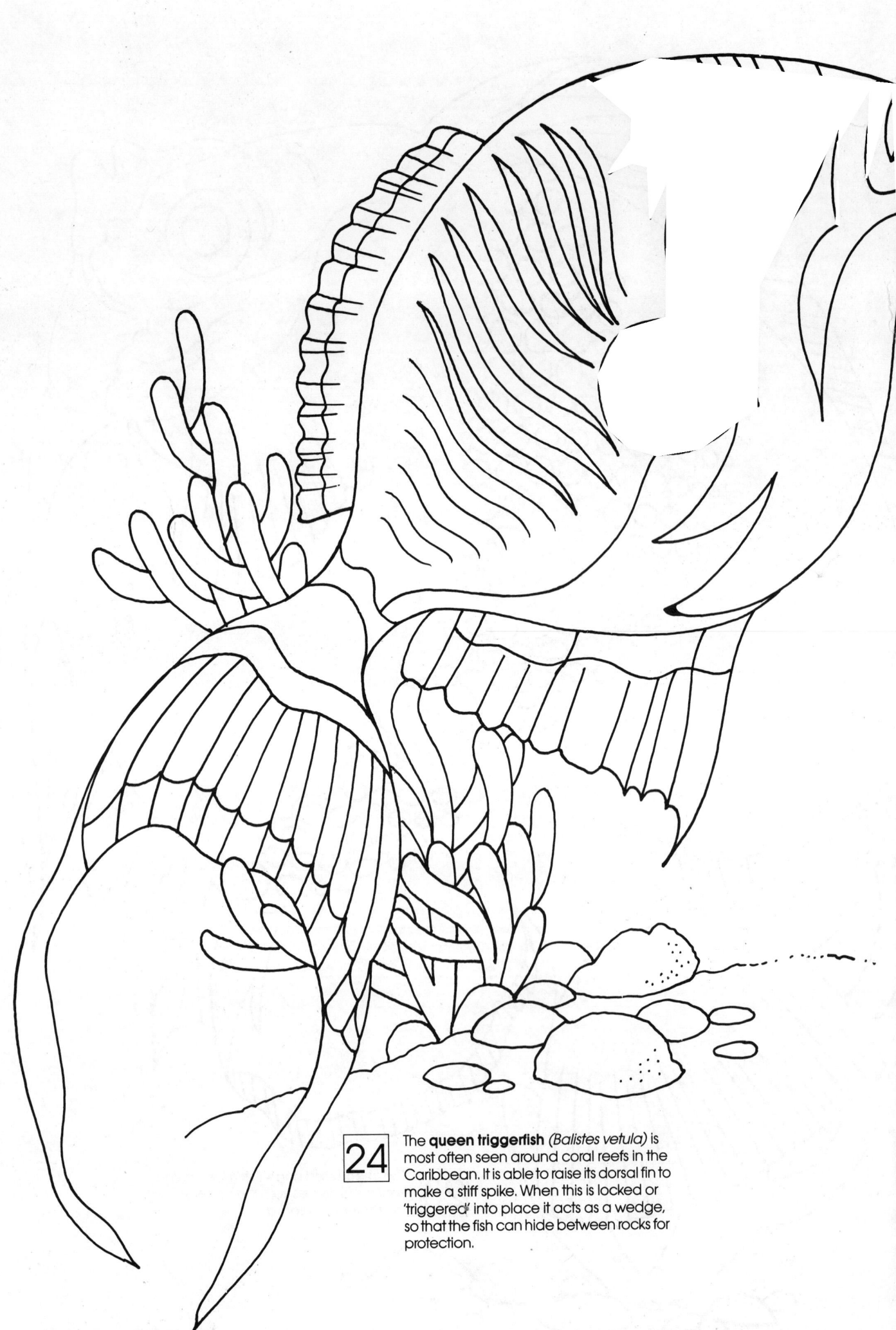

24 The **queen triggerfish** (*Balistes vetula*) is most often seen around coral reefs in the Caribbean. It is able to raise its dorsal fin to make a stiff spike. When this is locked or 'triggered' into place it acts as a wedge, so that the fish can hide between rocks for protection.